The History of

THE

V Q R

POETRY
SERIES

The History of Anonymity

POEMS BY JENNIFER CHANG

The University of Georgia Press   Athens and London

Published by the University of Georgia Press

Athens, Georgia 30602

www.ugapress.org

© 2008 by Jennifer Chang

Set in Minion Pro

by Graphic Composition, Inc., Bogart, Georgia

Printed digitally in the United States of America

Library of Congress Cataloging-in-Publication Data

Chang, Jennifer, 1976–

The history of anonymity : poems / by Jennifer Chang.

82 p. ; 22 cm. — (The VQR Poetry series)

ISBN-13: 978-0-8203-3116-4 (pbk. : alk. paper)

ISBN-10: 0-8203-3116-3 (pbk. : alk. paper)

I. Title.

PS3603.H3573H57 2008

811'.6—dc22

2007038596

British Library Cataloging- in-Publication Data available

For Albert, Constance, Marvin, & Sinmin

Contents

Acknowledgments

Grateful acknowledgment goes to the following publications, in which some of these poems first appeared: *Asian American Poetry: The Next Generation, Barrow Street, Beloit Poetry Journal, Best New Poets 2005, Blackbird, Black Warrior Review, Gulf Coast, MiPoesias, New England Review, Pleiades, Poetry Daily, Seneca Review, The New Republic, Verse Daily, Virginia Quarterly Review,* and *The Year's Best Fantasy and Horror 2006.*

"The History of Anonymity" received the 2004 Campbell Corner Poetry Prize and was first published on the Campbell Corner website.

This book would not have been possible without the hard questions and good faith of Charles Wright, Lisa Russ Spaar, Greg Orr, and Rita Dove: thank you. Thank you also to the many friends who read these poems and made them (and me) better. My love and gratitude to the Chang family for their exceptional exceptions and my alter-ego family, the Spaars, for keeping my glass full and my elbows off the table. Special thanks to Ted Genoways and the staffs of *Virginia Quarterly Review* and the University of Georgia Press for believing in this book.

I am indebted to University of Virginia's Creative Writing Program and Department of English, the Barbara Deming Memorial Fund, the Ludwig Vogelstein Foundation, The MacDowell Colony, the Djerassi Resident Artists Program, Bread Loaf Writers' Conference, Sewanee Writers' Conference, the Corporation of Yaddo, Asian American Writers' Workshop, and Kundiman for generous gifts of time, money, and community.

And, thank you, Aaron Baker: *you know it's true.*

Acknowledgments

The History of Anonymity

I had the fog's countenance
and it was good. It took me

to the seaside cliffs

where I watched the seaside from a crevice. Cold,

unctuous stone, I sat and saw

the darkness grow
and grow. Could this be

the afterworld?
I am in this world,

I am two parts water

to one part salt, I am

conciliatory

as a chair.

In The History

of Anonymity, the glacier longs to be water,

and each granule of salt

[handwritten annotations: "integrating (maybe colors)", "apperance?", "the condition of being anonymous", "Saying anonymas people don't want to be?"]

3

begs a lesser atom.   *We will know each other*

    less, the voice writes. *I am already*
    in this afterworld. *You will find me where the*

I am two parts . . .   *talking about insecurity*

   ——————

        Once,
I traveled to a shore

where I knew tide pools would form.
I loved the sea anemones, loose flowers

or creatures of all mouth,   moving more as water

    than as live things. Their mouths on my ankles,
    on my fingers, I wanted to be devoured

and could hear exhales

and inhales

whisper through water. Crouched, I saw this   as waving.

   So much

to the sea is seeing. I studied its

4

inconstancy,   its strange inability

to depart

for good. What if I said:

[handwritten: What is going on]

Stay off the shore. It is my shore   *[handwritten: pushing away the critisism from outside and in]*

and nothing shall enter it.   THE
END,   *finito, quod erat*

demonstrandum: never return.

See.

That simple.

---

from page 333 of The History of Anonymity –

The ocean swallowed my diary. It swallowed my words. I have
secrets from you. You with no name, do you love me who is

without a face? Or do you love me without   *[handwritten: (outside perspectives]*

a sound? In your arms, I am further and we are

one apparition—disperse

and sing

common image of a sea → no idea what it means

  quietly.   I believe,

  you are beginning   to understand me.

  Are we not   *sea has a negative connotation for the author*

  the same

  difference, the same   sums multiplied into an air

abandoned. Weren't you too

        born of an empty room? We lack

a bloom. Isn't that   where we are?

        Rootless. Love,   we are

        gone.

———————

  I swam to not drown: *(always on edge)*

                the difference between the two

  is one stroke.

6

The water had made me ill.

Submerged, my body—a wave, the sea's

disciple—was gone. My will,

a willing pawn.   The world was all

sea   long ago,

[handwritten: what is the sea supposed to mean]

in the beforeworld. I imagine

it was much like the afterworld.

Three thoughts and a wave could drag me to shore

or pull me under. The voice:

[handwritten: darkness, mental and physical]

To not be is to be free.

Beautiful pliability,
for once, I was without

questions, a mouth full of salt and seaweed,

kept afloat by heat

[handwritten: trying to use it to represent both outside world and herself]

and blood. One stroke against the undertow,

or one stroke for.

———

7

I have never liked walking
or listening. Both make me feel more alone.

I listened once
for a rarer bird. Too many gulls

grace this place,
their accompaniment of the tide's yes & no.

Anonymity is not a name
but an entrance. I won't tell you

where I've gone. Love pains us
with knowing. You want to turn the page,

uncertain by overthinking?

to define every open
vowel. O – that's where I begin

and end, O . . . no
gasp, please; read nothing into this. It is no music

the ocean makes. The sea,
the shore, whatever you choose

to call it, I won't be
there. I won't

———

                                    This tide pool
                              pockets five pink stones.

         At high tide, there will be none.
         There will not even be a pool.   And at low tide,

                    what then?

Perhaps anonymity is the ocean floor

without the ocean.

Then it must also be   the ground we walk on.

                              Those five pink stones

                                        and their life of subtraction,

their dustward ambition.   I would be good at that.

                                   The water had made me ill.

I sat in shallower ripples,

                                   counting dried-out starfish—

they died open-handed, golden—

Handwritten annotations:

(ocean represents something that covers or darkens) — covers secrets? (ground walk on, pink stones)

emotion — darkness eats them away

⟨ darkness eats away

9

I sat with two tight fists in my lap.

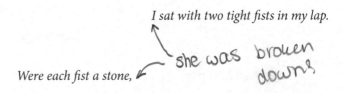 she was broken downs

Were each fist a stone,

I would know the ocean floor, I would

attend the ocean's departure. Often

I do not see myself

as different,

then the day comes   when I do not see myself at all. Shadows
limn my breath

and motion. What is

speaking: a voice or a mistake of hearing?

First, I was known,

_____

then unknown.

You don't believe me. You think

if there is a voice,

there is a soul, but you are young, your gestures suggest
your composition: stolen wings

of birds, laughable

accidents, and the kindest lies.   *what is going on*

They died brittle, holding nothing.

A starfish is a cruel hand,   will choke a sea urchin with its cruel clasp.

I have seen this many times.   Seen the sea urchin turn

describing the dangers of the unknown

anonymous, seen it limp

and lose its shell.   Six dried-out starfish

around a dried-out pool,   one   with each finger torn.

My voice

is always becoming another voice.

There were nights of evaporation: the ocean made a fog, fixed above,
and yet drifting into the next valley. Did the fog make an ocean there?
I won't say I am loneliest at night—

← repetition of this phrase

the water had made me ill—

but every night I saw   an entrance, and saw
the tides, at their highest, stand still.   Waves are waves
and wind their counterpoint.   And what am I?

← darkness is stable in the sense it is always there

from page 910 of <u>The History of Anonymity</u> –

Mostly, I have forgotten that world.

I had a face   then gave it up. The eyes
were gray. Or green, a color

       like a growl. I have   forgotten. In the
afterworld, every I

       is a we.   Does knowing this soothe you?
       Your longing

has a clean finish;

mine echoes its hollow chord,   is too frail.

Conversation with Owl and Clouds

Owl-night, moon-gone, my wherewithal
is yellow pine. Is trillium and unfurled frond.

Clouds,—a cantilever of the trees, vapor-
plied architecture of the ephemeral—teach me

the apparition-life, what tunes the branches'
nocturne off-key: how do bodies turn into

song? Glow of dust and sandstone light, stars
dropped like pebbles, like crumbs, heretofore

a fairy tale trail. Barn owl, secretive and out-
spoken, you spout two minds, a hiding place

and a traffic sign. What's this absence
you speak of? Nonsense-yakking *lost soul,*

lost soul, the self-question that grows—
Who what?—odd and old.

Build me up into the fog, into brevity
made beautiful, the wet-dressed disaster

that's rain, that's the storm-threat of forest fire.
I want to be ornate and ornery. More than

a vapor-child, a night's ward like the white
monkshood tucking under its bud, too shameful

to flower. I am hearing it: spring's first wild melt,
each drop trickling into the next, a minor

chord. So snow's gone, so how can I be
ice dissolving in water?

[handwritten: minor chords are associated with sadness]

Cloud me, sparrowing and bark-loose,
each season's dark ambition: a patient pattern

gone. O, I am hearing it: this say-nothing
noise, how the world's clamor-born and

sorrowful, tricked for loss, the silent purpling
of crocuses mouthing back at the owl:

I will not, and soon—

Hunger Essay

Thou turnest thy face away,
all things tremble and grow cold.
—Haydn, *Die Schöpfung*

He shows me a place in the forest
that sounds of creaking doors. *The young ones*

are growing. Each tree fights out
its earthwork. Branching around us, beneath us,

they are an imbroglio of roots—
a chokehold chorus.

From trunk to trunk, we do
the strangle, we do the wicked pole-dance.

He loves the birch's bone-thin pallor
and I watch him match his limbs

to the scrawniest wood.
He will not embrace the wider trees.

———

Blue-eyed towhead throbbing with falsetto:
Teurer Gatte, dir zur Seite,
schwimmt in Freuden mir das Herz.

He remembers our mother. I don't. She
was, he admitted, a weak soprano.
Dear husband, at thy side

my heart is bathed in rapture.
Blushing at *rapture,* he gestures, plays Mother's
Eve. Turns the duet solo, Adam gone

silent. *Der Abendhauch.* Because I won't
sing. Echoes the forest: *the evening wind.*

———————

Every puddle rivers with desire.
Paltry pools palming a leaf

long to pond.
What is that like? To not fit

one's true shape.
To be *less than.* Today he pretends

we've run away. I want to
kick him in the shins.

I want to say
Father orphaned us

before his time. Father
would thin the forest

[handwritten annotations in margin:]
theme of music → soprano minor chords

paints a picture music is a forest ↓ natural music

around our house, his axe
a second wife to marry.

His wife, an axe to bed. *A stepmother.*
I am a stepped child.

I am through
with chokecherries, through

with loam in my throat—
three weeks gone. Pussy-toed,

elegiac, he avoids the pools
and will not answer to *Brother.*

———

The Creation ends in love. He places
a hand on the well of my stomach, says
I am more hollow—his hand, a single

bone. We sleep on weather-brittle leaves, on
pine needles that fail to sting, and listen
to our bodies' private rumblings. We are

a thunder each. *The Creation* ends in
Alleluia! He fancies a garden
of cotton, a rock-sugar house that we'll

tear down with hunger. *But where will we live?*
We were born lost. The forest is our home.

The Forest on Second Thought

Never an *I*, never a question,
we answer without thinking

Yes, even to her, the girl
drinking reflection out of the stream.

We forgive the moss its tender rudiments
and forgive the bark

for falling and failing. Winter unveils
vast secrecy. The bare branch

shows no face, the wind's echo
no voice, but there is a trail

to every arrival, and she follows
what she believes.

We were a seed
then bursting made us many.

Made us tall. From above,
her head suggests raccoon, deer,

a body scavenging
its own shadow, an animal,

all the same. *Yes,*
this is the root to finding, here

[handwritten annotation:] you cannot see nature exactly but it is all around and you can see where it has been

are the strange tracks
of another that lead to a clearing,

to a shot of sunlight and recognition.
We know what wandering is.

We know how to follow,
and we stay.

is it an animal or no?

Apologia pro Vita Sua

I dreamt the ocean

dismantled our roof, and we two sleepers reckoned the cold apocalypse
like driftwood.

It was not a bad dream,

though the waves subtracted me, and you, solely sleeping,
rose: the ocean

makes a house of breathing. The waves salt one cheek

to parchment, your other cheek burns with light. You curl
into the tides, become your own

vessel, but where am I?

I see and cannot feel. The cuttlefish will never know you—what ink,
what mad swimmer—

the seabottom will never know you, Mister Drift,

Tidal Sleeper, may I dream myself the water that holds you,
the troublesome ripple that wakes you.

———————

*paints a
pic of the
sea as a
mystery waiting
to be uncovered*

The dark needs tending [*shows that even darkness needs effort to keep*]
I have a sorrow garden
flowers that grow wilder
        each night

So begins the letter I write   and will not send.

I will not give voice or ear to my words.
I have no right. Black plums

in a wooden bowl, the season's last fruit. August serves
sad heat. I study the wind to find
its autumn trace. I taste the plums slowly.

I did not understand then
your last letter   *I'm dumb*
dull   *I think I'll die from this*
ache   *or worse   live*

As a child, I would not eat the skin,   [← *likes pain?*]
but now I want the first sour bite, for it cuts
the flesh's sweetness. I line pits

along the windowsill. Three blue cars, unseen wrens
making bright noise of distance, a poem

I cannot finish. I think I'll die from this ache.

———

A memory:

I worked your hands, unburdened your palms
of their rough art. Your sandstone skin, my love, once mine.

Why did I stop? Why

diminish?
In the ocean,

I go bodiless, a breath and a thought

let loose in the waves. I see cormorants too wet
to fly. They stall

on rocks, learn shore. I am the water's cold heart,

cold eye. I am nothing.
I forgot to tell you

of poverty grass, of stubborn bloom.

Or that the path to this beach is unmarked

and many-stoned, and if I lie on the hot sand,
I lie on you.

If I did not lose my body to ocean,

I lost it to you. *Who is you?*

———————

Dear   we lived on
afternoon light   Dear
we shared one
*   white sheet*

Dear   you loved better
than I   your words
slow entrance into me
will love better   Dear

than I   the fruit of
*   errancy tastes bitter*
Dear is cold   please open
the window   my Dear   write

Pastoral

Something in the field is
working away. Root-noise.
Twig-noise. Plant
of weak chlorophyll, no
name for it. Something
in the field has mastered
distance by living too close
to fences. Yellow fruit, has it
pit or seeds? Stalk of wither. Grass-
noise fighting weed-noise. Dirt
and chant. Something in the
field. Coreopsis. I did not mean
to say that. Yellow petal, has it
wither-gift? Has it gorgeous
rash? Leaf-loss and worried
sprout, its bursting art. Some-
thing in the. Field fallowed and
cicada. I did not mean to
say. Has it roar and bloom?
Has it road and follow? A thistle
prick, fraught burrs, such
easy attachment. Stem-
and stamen-noise. Can I lime-
flower? Can I chamomile?
Something in the field cannot.

Obedience, or The Lying Tale

I will do everything you tell me, Mother.
I will charm three gold hairs
from the demon's head.
I will choke the mouse that gnaws
an apple tree's roots and keep its skin
for a glove. To the wolf, I will be
pretty and kind and curtsy
his crossing of my path.

The forest, vocal
even in its somber tread, rages.
A slope ends in a pit of foxes
drunk on rotten brambles of berries
and the raccoons ransack
a rabbit's unmasked hole.
What do they find but a winter's heap
of droppings? A stolen nest, the cracked shell

of another creature's child.
I imagine this is the rabbit way
and I will not stray, Mother,
into the forest's thick,
where the trees meet the dark,
though I have known misgivings
of light as a hot hand that flickers
against my neck. The path ends

at a river I must cross. I will wait
for the ferryman
to motion me through. Into the waves
he etches with his oar
a new story: a silent girl runs away,
a silent girl is never safe.
I will take his oar in my hand. I will learn
the boat's rocking and bring myself back

and forth. To be good
is the hurricane of caution.
I will know indecision's rowing,
the water I lap into my lap
as he shakes his withered head.
Behind me is the forest. Before me
the field, a loose run of grass. I stay
in the river, Mother, I study escape.

nature is all about
survival?

Innocence Essay

I only read in bed.
Father roosts on the edge of night,
waits for the book to drop.

I cross the hall
to become my mother
—we are one face—

and hide her ashes in a shell.
This is where Father wants to be.
Walnut, he calls me,

dad wants to be dead

—————

I only bite your hem. And it is true. It is
a tale Mother told
of the dark envelope. *Inside,* she said,
*were morsels of women, skin
as cold as sand.*
She did not know then
that her limbs were stitched
with air.

                    Holy remnant,
white stain on our sheet. Father,
I know, loves me.

—————

We pass in the garden.   How is *grass*
not *infinite passage?*
                                                I cannot look
but his fingertips
learn my lobe.   How is *forsythia* not

            gold gate that won't permit me?

Under my tree, I survey
the ineffable names of things.

I call this tree *Keeper*
though its fruits do not fall

to feed me.   *Walnut,*

            ——————

child of this mistaken wonder,
I am   *infanta,* Mother's
mirror——   half orphan,

half wife.   *I only bite your hem.*

Again. But *hem*   what is
                                                hem

            ——————

is what keeps me from the ground.

Or *hem*

is what divides word from sound.

    I read, and the book

        replaces the world.

I turn like pages.
           No,

the bed stations me,—

    ————

I surface, the climax, and gently
        conclude.—

the story is the trail.

Father wants a word with me. He sheds

        his light

around my bed, shifts
the room's dust.

        I do not budge.

I am in the margins.   Far

    ————

as she runs
from the castle

there are crumbs that will lead her back.

There are hunters
who will remember her

tucked into a fur mantle, clotted
with a season of leaves.

There are the bees who saw her
sobbing ponds. Their hive,
a curious dangle, an eye.   In this world,

the bees will talk.

I say *Go*   but the word whistles.

Go is a kettle
gone weird on the stove. *Go*
is Father's left brow, left hand,

left-behind shoe. Take these

to the garden and bury them
in the muddy roots of my tree

and they will grow blue hemlock.
They will grow old
                    like wallpaper vines.

What Mother called useful

————————

                    but ugly:

To each pin
tie a thumb-sized stone

and to each inch around your hem
lock a pin.   Wild winds

will never blow you over—
your skirt, your obedient whim.

                    Inside, you
know: to live the story

Creates image of
nature + death

————————

is to find an end.

Father, I know,

loves her.   In the garden,

Father buries

    the books I have finished,

the books I'll never read.   I am *Walnut,*

    the stone   locked in his mouth.

why is it italicized (handwritten annotation)

keeping him from dying? (handwritten annotation)

34

Sea Psalm

We see no ships at harbor. The sea is the sky's

gray mirror, and I am
                      in the dream of its plain reflection, the still water

        before a wave's ascent.

            What rise left in me   is left to follow you to shore.
Is an edge to narrow

what shoulders you—I cut the beach
                                    to bring you to water—

        and the odd wonder

you shoulder,   like a one-winged bird.

I want to call you *love,* as I want
                        to call the driftwood *house.*   Daily,

we age into erosion's remnants,
                            carving our lines

out of the coast, and I am learning to forgive
                                my longing to make strangeness

unstrange;   that our shadows, subsuming us,

do not complete us.

Where in the shell-mottled sand

will we make our ragged bed?   Now, *love,*

            the sea-wind salts our young skin,

our bodies turn to shell:

        let us be emptied
                    as this off-season shore,

            to be l•ved
'for what we lack.

Postscript

I lost the blue handle
of things, a paintbrush, our
ticket stubs.

I gathered gauze,
the cloud of you, curtains
ordinary as fog.

Books I stole from you,
I lost. The sinuous line
of these mountains

like a graph of doubt
rising. I thought
wrong—

the heart is
small and dull.
I heard the trees,

their birdless sighs.
I lost by accident:
noon's silence, the wonder

that forgetting makes.
You were gone
in the eyes, my origin.

Genealogy

This stream took a shorter course—
a thread of water that makes oasis

out of mud, in pooling,
does not aspire to lake. To river, leave

the forest, the clamorous wild.
I cannot. Wherever I am,

I am here, nonsensical, rhapsodic,
stock-still as the trees. Trickling

never floods, furrows its meager path
through the forest floor.

There will always be a root
too thirsty, moss that only swallows

and spreads. Primordial home, I am dying
from love of you. Were I tuber or quillwort,

the last layer of leaves that starts the dirt
or the meekest pond,

I would absorb everything.
I would drown. Water makes song

of erratic forms, and I hear the living
push back branches, wander off trail.

. . . those who speak most say nothing.

Say *sky*
and I sink into the dirt,
my body a bulb
waiting, waiting—

O sky, noise of being, blue
backdrop, without which
there is only the air
in my cupped palms.

I am asking a question about air and
sky. What is water
without the sea? Can the sand
marry me?

This voice, a purple scar
that may not flower. I can't stop
looking up just as I can't stop looking
down. Rub out the blue bud

and swallow its petal shreds:
if I eat what I kill,
will I rot as it does,
beautifully?

Slept

The thorns had hands. The fire stood still.
It will take a hundred years

to piece together a hundred dreams.
A room of ashes was a room outspun.

Mother says the heart is a wheel

and it will turn as I turn. Quickly.
Nightly.   I married the owl.

———————

I told her I could not walk,

the walls circled my steps. I told her
my flesh became stone   and I did not

bleed blood, but sound.
What sound?   I could not describe it;

it was voiceless

and low. But it was not.
Mostly I was not   alone in my solitude.

My breath became the ghost of me

or the ghost of an old man
I'd long forgotten,

                        a midnight grandfather.

Pages of thoughts, they were not mine,
            though my hand mastered

their language. I told her

            I cannot howl winsomely
like vixens.
                        Like thieves. I wandered the forest,

fingering every loose twig,
but I was sleeping. My hand,

good as air, was sleeping.

            ————

In my sleep, I wrote the field guide:
red-winged dream, tufted dream.

One was of salt,

            one without hunger—a forest

of three-leaved trees.
I thought I knew everything.

My bed sat alone amongst the sassafras.
A fox, mid-pace and mid-bark, stopped

statue-like on a patch of moss.

      I was watcher,

or maker.   Yellow-bellied
dream, mourning dream.

Each thing I saw: a seed to a self.

Inside a girl stirred restless as rain.
I could not see her. I only grew.

Mother says when the basket's full,
it is time to come home.

      ————

Asleep, I lived

      in silence, but in light.

What if waking   were a room
black as the mind? Hornbilled dream,

Steller's dream. And the body,

a darkness   there is no memory of.

Estuary

My house faced an estuary.
I looked for where ocean tide
instructed river flow.
I was more river, pliant
to the sea, and did no roving.
Supple as current, and as reckless, I was
a loose believer.
My face, an estuary.
My river-mouth. Ocean-eyed.

————

Mornings were a drowned city. Gulls
fell from the fog, their voices
trailing chords of hunger.

They say absence culls the wayward,
that the derelict leaf
soon ashes and is air.

Who says?

Well,
I heard it said. And, sensing my own
diminishment, know it.

————

Color of water—
not blue, not clarity.
Heard the loon
brooding regret,
or caution: *The darkest*
pools of water
form the sky's silhouette.

———————

I was not good. The house sank,
the soggy bank would not hold.
A spirit rocking like a boat
took me to this between place.
Took me for goodness—

I mistook. No, misspoke.
The poverty grass

flowering in the dunes. True, what is
ruinous
is also vital. When I swim to the estuary,
I will not know where I am.

———————

I chased the breakers, their compass of *come*
and *come again.*

Believe me,
the bay mothered the cove, and both
are outlet and inlet: *Let down,*

let go.

Where the swallowed voice
becomes the choking voice.
In the estuary, I saw a face of silent answer.

And the night illuminated the night

No one sees how night fades you.

Not the stars' lambent sparks—

born blind, light years gone.
Even you don't see

                   the black line of yourself,
the vanishing

you slowly come to, a shadow gift.

You're the kind
who walks into a forest
and becomes

              indistinguishable from the trees.
Find a ghost reflection

in the field
flooded
with the moon's graylight—why is splendor

     so ordinary?

Be branch and dirt,
be stiff as your oak skin, oak heart.

No one led you here,
only dark curiosity, the trail

trained to lose you.
Inside, you have a longing

but it is hard.

                You could have been odd,

a fiddlehead: embryonic
and translucent, it waits to unfurl,

to spore. You could have been a white thread
tangled in the grass,

a thing that feigns glowing,
a thing that feigns.

This Corner of the Western World

Dark thing,
make a myth of yourself:

all women turn into lilacs,

all men grow sick of their errant scent.
You could learn

to build a window, to change flesh
into isinglass, nothing

but a brittle river, a love of bone.

You could snap like a branch—*No,*

this way, he says, and the fence
releases the forest,

and every blue insect finds an inch of skin.
He loves low voices, diffidence

on the invented trail,

the stones you fuck him on. Yes
to sweat's souvenir, yes to his fist

in your hair, you bite

because you can. Silence
rides the back of your throat,

his tongue, your name.

End Note

Before words, there was the language of the mark.
We moved a stick along the dirt and drew
a line to the end. Our wild flickers
ink-streaked a page, symbols like the stars'
orphaned radiance giving more light
than reason. He holds out a hand: *What do you see?*
Skin of absolution, there is nothing. I wrote S
before I learned the letter, and when he warned
Be silent as the "e" in house, I woke our father.
He had outgrown me with his name.
More wisp than dart, the sun rarely finds us
in the forest: he holds the fruit—I see
a breath vanishing—he knows the spell:
I live for a word, wordlessly.

Postscript

We did not marry, cross, or fasten
forest with field. We split—

lightening-struck trees, splintered
raw, a natural Y,

two arms of wanting. Love,
we broke

and found the stones coreless,
gone wild with error,

gone. Tonight the field disentangles
the night's creature

concert, insect hymn. Holy shine
that webs the sky

unwebs our sight: I have a vision
you don't see,

a mind's pastoral, not secret
but unreachable

by road, sea, or thought: the lamps
sprout gorgeously,

the wheat is strange. You don't see
sorrow burrowing

in coupled roots, how the forest
finds its way

down here, bone-cold dirt, dendritic
tangle, my wish

to grow old in shadow—must I
die alone?

We did not unearth this rude radical,
we burst.

A Move to Unction

The sign reads:

Unction—
> *a sanctuary for the solitudes.*
> Yes. I am one

too. A solitude gone
blank, the husk of my life
narrowing

into a blade. I have no
neighbors here and my neighbors
have none too.   I will pour

last night's storm
over my skin,
> catch it all

in every pore.
This rain is grief-thick.
I used to wake in my childhood home

and want my family to burn, with me
as the flame's blue dart.
They are embers now

or could have been.
Sister pooling on the kitchen tile,
                    her formless anger

forming my current burden.   Don't I lie
each time I promise
I did not leave her behind?

Swindled, I left everything.

A town with remote reception
and hollow hills that sway like elms,
          Unction blooms one vast zero,

a mirror of my ramrod heart

lost in the collection plate's steely face.

I'm looking out a new window
only to realize it is no different: a roof's

hypotenuse, a one-armed tree, the sky

a white enormity. I hide
          only to find myself too much.

So where's
safety, the trail

that led me here,
that will lead me back?   *Unction* hums

parts of a song I once knew—it's
          in the wind, like a ribbon shredded loose and

feathered—I'm uncouth,
          indecipherable—*Wanting all I have lost,*

I have lost nothing.
But I have lost everything.

I float in. I float out.

Mother favored her.
I tell her this
and she does not believe it.

(This was one of our last conversations.
Her voice, a liquid tremolo
trying not to boil.)

Mother had bones
of wood beams. *No,* Sister says,
steel—she was a skyscraper. That was why

Father left her, never warm enough.
Too far from the ground.
Her hands were saucers,

tiny and round, holding
a teacup, sometimes a spoon
for stirring sugar. This maudlin

description sullies Sister who
silently spills away:
                                    the part of the memory

that leaves me cold
as when it happened.
Strong rooms make strong families

and we lived between a creek
and a cloud.

> What does that mean?

Today I am writing postcards:

Unction is like no place at all!
My tomatoes appear like lightbulbs!
The milk is white honey! I forgive you!

I go to the backyard and one by one toss them off the cliff.

I remember her, a bowl of water.

Here in *Unction,* thirst
is currency. I have wealth

and I have greed, my head
a pool of waves I drown in daily. I see

the walls wave too, fretting
ignorant sheets

of light. Reflection, nothing
but

a different way of looking,
I think. Or, isn't shadow

a black water, the shallow ink
we can't dive into

but want to? I remember her,
a bowl of water

I spun my loose
buttons in—a sort of

tiddlywinks—until
she spilled out and broke

the bowl. A burst
that rang like bells. Who

wiped her off the floor?
Where did she pour? Jars,

thimbles, a porcelain basin.
She ended the game. But couldn't she,

like me, have been a band
in the spectrum? A violet murmur

to my red haze? O,
she swam and she swims, treads

against currents I can't find, to the deep
where even light drowns

and water's the one uncertainty
to count on. Somewhere deeper

we will forget our faces. Sister,
here's the dress

I hand down to you—lace of algae
and brine, a sea urchin's

limy shell—hand it down
farther.

Today the action is in the clouds:

Mother holds a bowl of water, drifts
languidly across the blue room.
                    She does not know where
            Sister is, that what remains of our family
is in her hands.

Does Mother ask for me?   I once began
                a letter to Sister. There was no reply.   But I think
the postal service here is poor;   no one gets letters
                    in *Unction.*

A cloud overflows.   It is a puddle
            widening into a bay.   Sister, I always believed,
could be an ocean. She had a talent
                    to be at once weightless
and sinking, a pawn of the waves
                but also the tide.

                        She would irritate me,
I am ashamed to admit, speaking to me
                from underwater so I could not discern
gurgle from word. Her language of ripples
                    was no language at all. Though I pretended to
know her phrases—

I am swallows, beads, and trickles   *I've caught the summer*
heat under my arm   *and you are a worried light*   *but my deepest pain*
         is evaporation   *you fret too much*
for articulation   *or the winter chafing me to hardness*

     —all lies I'll label imagination. What I would do
         for a word. Mother, her cloud,
   darkens, wants the bowl to pour out.

In the night, I seek a meaning before I sleep.

A sister is a solace.
A daughter
is a mother's dotage.
To be either is to deny a self:

     I am not enough
as part of something, I want to be
one thing. So then, what is a mother
if not a source?   Ours glowed

and glowered, showed us the dark
as a gallery of doors
to more doors.   A mirror too,
for I have darks I follow

and fetch. How am I any good
if I am not   attentive? In the ground,
a fluted tulip is unborn. Nothing new. Yes,
nothing new, but there—

Sister strums her bones and cries
like a water-harp, tired
of her partness,   apart
again and departing. What

does Mother want from us?
Sister does not think the tulip flowers
without the bulb. She's right, but
who needs to see the bulb?

I like the petals red, the four-part
stamen more *t* than *x*. It is all wait
and wilt. In the ground,
        there is a secret to grief

which is only a door
with a face drawn on the threshold.
This is who stole   Mother's spine
and splinter, leaving her

a morsel of dirt and a filthy hand
to raise at her children.   A hand
is a door to days I can't see, older
than seeking. What Sister and I were born

of,—   a questioning stem is
the filament swallowing
        the form—what we were
born to be,   rooms disguised as doors.

If there is no memory, it did not happen.

Mother took us
and locked us in the basement.
Sister has no memory

of this. She was, at the time,
small enough to close in a cupboard.
But the basement

was the house's dank hollow,
where the groans grew,
where we kept our yams and onions cool.

We sank into the top step
afraid to go all the way down;
there was a clucking or a whir

—*You're making it
up.* —a sound that thinned us out.
Even then I needed glasses

but would not admit it. I see the memory
in my head, only blurs. *You read
something strange in those blurs,*

*you read a story
and not the truth.* My arms slowly
disappeared so that as I grew older

I could feel nothing. *Self-pity! Whose*
arms disappear? You were simply born
that way. Mother's rages

tore off our skins. Sometimes
I was glad for myopia. How awful
we must have looked to be limbless,

skinless, and without even the vigor
to butter our toast. We ate bread dry,
like cardboard, no, we let it go

soggy in its hard heat. *There was no*
toaster, no oven. Mother made wonderful
salads and after Father left, we each

had a dozen kernels of corn at dinner.
Who looked more like Mother? A question
that gave me purpose then. I did not want

her temperament, but I think
she had a lovely face, a wedge of moonglow
and a catalpa leaf. So I looked

carefully. I squinted because those days,
Mother was in love with our poverty
and had the celerity

of a blender. *Oh, the blurs again.* And Sister,
in adolescence, had a spinning jenny
way, a movement like grass

on a windy day. *Did you see anything?*
I saw what I saw:
Sister became watery.

How was I swindled if I was the swindler?

When Sister could still speak, she would say

      We were swindled!

                then spill away, forgetting her cup and spoon,
to feign a foppish drowning.

By what? I wondered.
We owned nothing and knew,
secretly, that everything was a trick. Perhaps
she said

           We were swindling!

Taking turns to knock on the front door,
         the other would cry out *Mother, Father's come back!*

A groan that rang like delight from her,
then blank
seeing no one on the porch, Sister or me
sniggering in the shrubbery.

It was sometimes easier to be ugly
than unhappy.
         Sister pooled at Mother's bedside
and took it all, the vehement spit,
the sloppy sobbing—

We were swindled! Again.

Or was it *spindled*?   I caught her once

hugging the mop.

I was no comfort to her. She should have said

I was swindled!

Were we then

a family of swindlers?   Or a swindled family?

What I feed on will save me.

Always a
squall inside—

my chest inflates
from the booming.
Joints like iron bells, O,
the bone-chimes, timpani
of limbs.

I want to wake to only air.

       Only air
          and nothing else.

A silent hymn, I imagine,
winds through the grass.

An ache's loud throbbing,
but am I not

a house of quiet chambers?

A stain. A sister.
Such a shout.

I have finished my oysters and dropped the shells:
they are teeth chattering loose
on the floor, foolish

without a mouth
to form words. I feast
to not hear the noise,

a firmament of chewing,
the rubbery flesh
a resistance I wish I had. It is a nourishment,
it is a hungry lesson.

What the landscape works for is what I have left.

Is *Unction*

the cloud that covers
                    or the cloud that passes?

A mystery, even to me.
            Am I a vapor in a vapor town

            and is Sister's memory a dew bead
forgotten on a grass blade?   White spaces, white fillers, the sky

            is the caulk that frames the cloud. Here, with my arms
I imitate the birches' bleached silhouettes

            to become the thinnest grove,   tracing the wind
                    that dissipates

and shapes.   I am branched
                        and branchless in

this ecstasy of absence—I swallow air

            until my hunger is   an insatiable question.

Then Sister was the empty bowl?
Then I was the futile drain?

            I wish her on a hill   somewhere far

from the cold chambers Mother made.   A night

                    that rang like rage—how

        do I go on?   The walls trembling, or was that

a twist of light?
Mother was killing herself
or killing us.   No,

            it's not that simple.
                            She held the blade in her small palms

not knowing how to stop the rain.   Our roof a snare drum,

        it had been raining for weeks—my dreams
were of swamps and drowning,   I scorned the shower,

hid from the tub,   fearing the faucet,   that rain
        should come inside.   White spaces, white fillers, the sky—

            How could I stop the knocking

on the window? Sister slept in the pantry; she believed

            in cyclones.   And Mother wailed with the thunder.

Really she did not know what to do
with two saucer-eyed daughters—
                            one licking floor dust,
                            the other coiled in the sheets—

so dragged us by our necks to the backyard
        and dipped us in the goldfish pond,   wailing

with the thunder.   The pond was black, the fish were gone.
        I wish her

drying on the clothesline, white as the shirts
        that fly in this wind.   Through the splash,

I could see Sister close her eyes

and swallow water, her mouth

        open as a door.   Though Mother had our hair
in fists, though I choked on rain and pond,

            a furious qualm—Sister so quiet
        she silenced the storm.

                            The clouds
    are sinking down to me—could I be what holds

the mist?   Enough of this.   I avoid
        to avoid.   *Don't I?*

I follow the day's inclination and find myself returned.

No, that cannot be.   I did not want

her drowning, to shape myself into
one grief. I said to Sister,   *Enter the house*

but build your own. A stronger skeleton, a roof

of your own choosing.   But what
could she choose? What could she choose?

Mother clung to the failed light of stars
so nightly we read by her fists, straining the page,

straining . . .   This was no life
was what struck me.   I construct walls

an arm's length from truth
and they surround me with their eggshell gleam.

I want to stop being
the column that keeps the ceiling

from falling.   But I am afraid, even now,

remembering how afraid I was then. And did Sister dissolve
seeing I had no hope? *Mother,* see,

must be a question or a demand. Mother curled
in a bed of our torn hair,   steam rising around her

or for her. Not a demon, not a witch, but broken too early
to ever grow, her private hurts winking

        as if to say *Haven't we met*
before?   Open the door and there she stood,
        her mouth an endless ringing. A howl

or an outcry? *A hoot,* Sister said, pretending

not to care that Mother wanted us deaf, dumb,
and maybe a little dead. *Ha ha, Mama!*   By then,

neither of us slept anymore, huddling in the closet
like lint. Open the door

and we were a frantic scatter.   *This is no game,* I whispered
in Sister's ear. She was a silent ripple, mute

to me, eyes shut by their own water.   She was not

listening.
I did not save her. I saved myself.

        Each night I am moved by the darkness here. Is it a black
silence or a silken sheath of wind? I know of nothing

but the wounds opening even as I close.

Each thing is two things.

A line thin as thread
plucks a mute note.
Why should a line
not have a song? Why
should a line
be a wire? I am
thinking only of what
matters now. I cannot
love anyone if I do not
know why I should or who
could love me. Or
Sister had asked, *How can you*
be happy being a weed's seed?
But all seeds grow something.
A line made loose
by bad weather
does not lose itself to storm,
keeps the lineness
of a ligament, which is a word
like any other. So I grow
a tin roof, a wall of stone,
stalks made strong by grief
blooming the cement bud
I'll call rose. It is what
I want it to be, even if
I must lie. Perhaps Sister knows
our tears are glue. This, too, a line.
So the silence is a sylph
and so we will.

I am in Unction now.

All my life   I have known
Mother stood beside a hole.

Some people carry shadows,
bad weather, but she nursed

an emptiness none of us could fill.
She liked   the pain of space

and would not let Father walk with her.
She swore she had no reflection

so our house was without
a single looking-glass. I held my hands

to my face and saw there was not much
to see anyway.   Sister cried

into her pillow
and sought a teary mirror. At night,

I said to her, we must keep   ourselves
from looking   for what isn't there. Even then,

I recognized my hypocrisy. I find everywhere
Mother's space,   the hole

deepened by regret. It is where starlings
hide their stolen eggs.   It is where

Father dropped his spectacles, took
the wrong step.   And I do not stop

to look in, to search for a dime
I have been missing twenty years.

What else have I lost? If I write a list,
I will lose the thing,   the desire

for retrieval.   So I tell myself. *Unction*
is a town of glass, not an escape.

          I am tired of the past.
I am so tired.

Can something broken be so beautiful?

Cross-legged in the backyard, I gaze
out over the cliff. *Unction*

                              is a town of vapor
and a white stillness cloaks
every morning thought. My bulky spine, my cumbersome

skull, I wait
                    to disintegrate.   *Shame's*

a puddle, Sister once said. But she never said that.

She had no gift
for language and her voice is the one thing

I cannot remember.   I cannot see the lines

that mark the clouds.   *I take the shape*
of what holds me   only to become its weight. I am now
resting in Mother's palm   feeling the cold stretch

of pain, I am water
over a rock, I am   flow.   Perhaps she murmured

as a lake lulls its evening lapping.   How long

the length from day to night. *Nothing's*
        a lullaby—why not nap?   It is too soon,
I speak into the sky and pluck a blade of grass.

She is not dead, but frozen
like a white glass.   This too

I cannot know.   *Sister, my silence*
     is my sustenance.   *You left me, yes,*
but didn't I leave as well?
Can I live in a lie?   This is the rain

that makes the puddle.   *Not frozen, as you*
imagine, but afloat . . .   I raise my arms

into the air. I would like to reach for something.

Notes

"Conversation with Owl and Clouds" contains phrases from *King Lear.*

Lines 14–15, 18–19, and 22–23 in "Hunger Essay" are excerpts from Joseph Haydn's opera *Die Schöpfung* (in English: *The Creation*), whose libretto is by Gottfried van Swieten.

"*. . . those who speak most say nothing*" derives its title from *The Confessions of St. Augustine.*

"*And the night illuminated the night*" derives its title from *The Lover's Discourse* by Roland Barthes.

Made in United States
North Haven, CT
06 August 2023

40010932R00064